A Robbie Reader

What's So Great About...?

ANNIE OAKLEY

Jim Whiting

P.O. Box 196
Hockessin, Delaware 19707
Visit us on the web: www.mitchelllane.com
Comments? email us: mitchelllane@mitchelllane.com

Mitchell Lane PUBLISHERS

Printing   2   3   4   5   6   7   8   9

A Robbie Reader/What's So Great About . . . ?

Amelia Earhart	Anne Frank	**Annie Oakley**
Christopher Columbus	Daniel Boone	Davy Crockett
Elizabeth Blackwell	Ferdinand Magellan	Francis Scott Key
Galileo	George Washington Carver	Harriet Tubman
Helen Keller	Henry Hudson	Jacques Cartier
Johnny Appleseed	Paul Bunyan	Robert Fulton
Rosa Parks	Sam Houston	

Library of Congress Cataloging-in-Publication Data
Whiting, Jim, 1943–
    Annie Oakley / by Jim Whiting.
        p. cm. — (A Robbie Reader. What's so great about . . . ?)
    Includes bibliographical references and index.
    ISBN 1-58415-477-2 (library bound)
    1. Oakley, Annie, 1860–1926. 2. Shooters of firearms — United States — Biography — Juvenile literature. 3. Women entertainers — United States — Biography — Juvenile literature. I. Title. II. Series.
    GV1157.O3W45 2007
    799.3092 — dc22

                                                                                          2006006114
ISBN-13: 9781584154778

ABOUT THE AUTHOR: Jim Whiting has been a remarkably versatile and accomplished journalist, writer, editor, and photographer for more than 30 years. He has written and edited about 200 nonfiction children's books. His subjects range from authors to zoologists and include contemporary pop icons and classical musicians, saints and scientists, emperors and explorers. Representative titles include *The Life and Times of Franz Liszt*, *The Life and Times of Julius Caesar*, *Charles Schulz*, *Charles Darwin and the Origin of the Species*, *Juan Ponce de Leon*, *Robert Fulton*, and *The Scopes Monkey Trial*. He lives in Washington State with his wife and two teenage sons.

PHOTO CREDITS: Cover—Getty Images; pp. 1, 3, 14, 16, 20, 24—Library of Congress; p. 4—Buffalo Bill Historical Center, Cody, Wyoming, P.69.961, detail; p. 6—Buffalo Bill Historical Center, Cody, Wyoming, Vincent Mercaldo Collection, P.71.368.3, detail; p. 8—Buffalo Bill Historical Center, Cody, Wyoming, P.69.1161, detail; p. 12—Buffalo Bill Historical Center, Cody, Wyoming, Vincent Mercaldo Collection, P.71.362.1, detail; p. 18—Buffalo Bill Historical Center, Cody, Wyoming, Gift of D.F. Barry, P.69.2125, detail; p. 22—Buffalo Bill Historical Center, Cody, Wyoming, Gift of Guthrie L. and Euradean Moses Dowler, the great niece of Annie Oakley, P.69.1594, detail; p. 10—Sharon Beck; p. 26—The Sculpture Center.

TABLE OF CONTENTS

Words in **bold** type can be found in the glossary.

Annie Oakley loads shells into a shotgun. She would have used a gun similar to this around her Ohio home to shoot game. She quickly acquired a reputation as an excellent shot.

A Shooting Match

Frank Butler knew his way around guns. He made his living traveling around the country and entering contests. Local people challenged him to shooting matches. He always won.

One day in 1881, he was in Greenville, Ohio. The people he met there said their local shooter was very good. They wanted to set up a contest. Frank accepted. He felt confident that he would win again. However, the men who organized the contest left out one detail about his opponent.

Frank said, "I almost dropped dead when a little slim girl in short dresses stepped out to the mark with me."

Frank Butler was one of the country's top marksmen when he met Annie. The two were almost inseparable from the start.

His other opponents had been men. This new rival was very tiny. She was only about five feet tall.

Frank lost. "I was a beaten man the moment she appeared for I was taken off guard," he said later. He said the final score was 23 to 21.

For the young woman, that shooting match was the start of a public career that would last for more than 40 years. She became one of the most famous women in the world.

Her name was Annie Oakley.

Phoebe Ann Moses discovered her shooting talent when she was only eight. After a troubled childhood, she found fame and fortune as the crack shot Annie Oakley.

A Difficult Childhood

Annie Oakley had a different name when she was born on August 13, 1860. Her name was Phoebe (FEE-bee) Ann Moses (some sources say her last name was Mosey). Her parents were Jacob and Susan Moses. She had three older sisters. The other girls called the new baby Annie. The family lived in Darke County, Ohio.

Annie's father died before she was six. He left behind a big rifle. Her mother ordered all her children to leave the rifle alone. Annie disobeyed her. She took the gun outside one day when she was eight. She bagged a squirrel with her very first shot. Annie later said she never knew where her shooting ability came from. It always seemed natural to her.

Annie was born in Darke County, Ohio. She lived there until when she was about 21. After that she traveled around the United States and even to Europe.

It was hard for her mother to support the family. When Annie was ten, she went to live at the Darke County **Infirmary**. Many elderly people and orphans lived there. It was a sad place, because the people there felt **abandoned**. One day a farmer came to the infirmary. He wanted a girl to help out at his house. She would do chores and other tasks. He seemed nice. He promised that Annie would have time for herself. She could even to go school.

The man was lying. He and his wife were harsh and cruel. Annie had no time to herself. She cooked. She cleaned. She took care of the animals. Even with all her hard work, she was beaten. One night the man threw her out into the snow. She nearly froze to death. In later life, she never told anyone the name of the family. She called them "the wolves."

Finally she was able to escape. She went back to the infirmary. She helped out the family that was in charge. She was very responsible, and they treated her well.

When she was 15, she finally returned home. Her mother had remarried. Now Annie could hunt to her heart's content. She shot **game** for her family. She also supplied restaurants with plenty of meat for their customers.

She gained a reputation as an excellent shot. Her reputation led to the shooting match with Frank Butler.

Annie poses with some of the many awards she received for shooting. This pose is similar to one of her most famous tricks. She held the rifle as shown. She grasped a mirror in her other hand. She used the mirror to aim at targets behind her.

Starting Out

Most men in that **era** would have been **humiliated** by losing to a girl. Frank Butler wasn't. He was impressed with Annie's shooting talent. He was even more impressed with her as a person. In fact, he fell in love with her. He began seeing her as often as he could. Then he proposed to her. According to their marriage license, the wedding took place in 1882.

Annie became Frank's partner when he gave public shooting shows, but she wanted one thing to be different. She wanted a different last name. She decided on Oakley. No one knows why she made this decision.

Chief Sitting Bull of the Sioux Indian nation is most famous for defeating Colonel George Armstrong Custer at the Battle of Little Bighorn. The victory was short-lived. Within a year or two, most of the Indians who fought there were living on government-established reservations.

Annie Oakley became an audience favorite. She would come on stage in a long dress. She looked just like any other young woman—until she started shooting. Frank taught her many shooting tricks. One of her favorites was shooting a lit cigarette from Frank's mouth.

After a while, Frank decided to become her full-time manager. Still, life was a struggle. To make a living, Frank and Annie had to travel to many different towns and cities. It was expensive and exhausting.

In 1884, Annie met Sitting Bull, a **Sioux** chief. He was famous because he had defeated Colonel George Custer at the Battle of Little Big Horn. He gave her an Indian name. It was Watanya Cecila, and it meant "Little Sure Shot." Sitting Bull even wanted to adopt her. Politely, Annie declined.

William F. Cody spent most of his early life on the Western frontier. He became a Pony Express rider when he was just 15. He became known as Buffalo Bill because he hunted buffalo to feed the men working on the transcontinental railroad.

Becoming Famous

In 1885, Annie and Frank joined Buffalo Bill's Wild West Show. The owner, William F. Cody, had become famous as a buffalo hunter. His nickname was Buffalo Bill. Cody said his Wild West Show showed life on the western **frontier**. In the show were cowboys on bucking broncos, Indians in war paint, Pony Express riders, outlaws robbing stagecoaches, covered wagons, and hundreds of horses, elk, buffalo, and other animals. The **spectacular** show was very realistic.

Annie was almost unknown when she joined the show. She became one of its most famous acts. She fired pistols with both hands. She shot while lying on her back. Sometimes

Sitting Bull and Buffalo Bill Cody were among the most famous people in the Wild West Show. Cody had a reputation for treating the Indians in his troupe with dignity and respect. He liked to show whites and Indians living in harmony.

the target was behind her and she'd have to find it using a mirror.

In one of their fanciest tricks, Frank would stand on a chair holding a four-inch disk. Annie would have her back to him. At a signal, he'd drop the disk. She'd have less than half a second to whirl around, spot the disk, aim her gun, and fire. No matter what type of shot she tried, she hardly ever missed.

Sitting Bull watches as Annie practices her shooting. Annie had a great deal of natural talent, but she wouldn't have been as successful as she was without long hours of practice.

The Wild West Show added the Congress of Rough Riders of the World in 1893. The new act featured military maneuvers and horsemen from foreign countries, including the Cossacks of the Caucasus, a region in Russia.

Annie's personality added a lot to her success. She always smiled and laughed. She looked like she was having fun. This attitude carried over into the audience.

The Wild West Show toured the United States. It was a great success. People happily paid the cost of admission to see all the acts. For those who could not pay, Annie often gave free tickets to her shows. Today, many people refer to free tickets as "Annie Oakleys."

The show even made two tours in Europe. Annie met England's Queen Victoria. Later, the two women exchanged some letters.

During one of the tours, Annie found out how famous she had become. A **rumor** had spread that she had died. The story made headlines around the world. People were very happy to learn that it was a mistake.

In 1893, Annie and Frank bought a home in Nutley, New Jersey. They lived there part of the year. The rest of the year they toured with the Wild West Show.

In her later years, Annie spent a lot of her time teaching girls and young women to shoot. She felt it was important that they be able to protect themselves. She and Frank also gave lessons to U.S. soldiers who were involved in World War I.

Later Life

Annie stayed with the Wild West Show until 1901, when she was injured in a railroad accident. She had to take time off to recover, but it didn't end her career. She put on local shooting exhibitions.

She suffered a different kind of injury in 1903. This one wasn't to her body. It was to her reputation. Two newspapers in Chicago reported that she had stolen a man's pants. To be thought of as a thief was bad enough. Even worse, the newspapers claimed that she used money she found in the pants to buy illegal drugs. Many newspapers across the nation printed the false story.

BUFFALO BILL'S WILD WEST·
CONGRESS, ROUGH RIDERS OF THE WORLD.

MISS ANNIE OAKLEY,
THE PEERLESS LADY WING-SHOT.

Buffalo Bill took full advantage of Annie's popularity in advertising his Wild West Show. It was highly unusual for a woman to shoot as well as, if not better than, a man. The wing-shot the poster refers to is hitting a flying game bird or clay target.

Annie was outraged. She had spent her entire life building a solid reputation. Most of the newspapers printed **retractions**, admitting the story wasn't true. Their retractions were not enough to erase what they had done. Annie

sued them. Her reputation was very important to her. She spent most of the next seven years clearing her name.

In 1911, Annie went back on tour for three years. Then she and Frank settled in Cambridge, Maryland. Annie began a project. She taught other women how to shoot. She thought it was so important that she gave her lessons for free. When the United States entered World War I in 1917, she and Frank taught American soldiers how to shoot better.

After the war, movies became especially popular. Annie thought about going to Hollywood. In 1894, she had appeared in one of inventor Thomas Edison's test movies. It lasted just 80 seconds. She had also been the star of two popular stage plays.

In 1922, she was involved in a serious car crash. It greatly affected her health. She died on November 3, 1926. Frank was overwhelmed by grief. He died just a few weeks later. They were buried next to each other. The gravesite is only a few miles from where Annie was born.

A bronze statue of Annie stands in her hometown of Greenville, Ohio. Greenville also hosts an annual Annie Oakley Festival. It is held during the last full weekend in July. Naturally, it includes a shooting contest.

During her life, Annie Oakley was noted for her generous attitude. She donated a great deal of her time and money to help others.

She was one of the first American female **media** superstars. She served as a role model for girls and young women. She encouraged women to live up to their potential. She would say, "Aim at a high mark and you will hit it. No, not the first time, nor the second and maybe not the third. But keep on aiming and keep on shooting for only practice will make you perfect. Finally, you'll hit the Bull's-Eye of Success."

That is excellent advice for anyone, boy or girl.

CHRONOLOGY

1860   Phoebe Ann Moses (or Mosey) is born on August 13.

1881*   Annie defeats Frank Butler in a shooting match.

1882*   Annie marries Frank Butler.

1884   Annie meets Chief Sitting Bull, who gives her the nickname Little Sure Shot.

1885   Annie joins Buffalo Bill's Wild West Show.

1894   Annie stars in one of Thomas Edison's first films.

1901   Annie is injured in a train accident and retires from the Wild West Show.

1903   Newspapers print false stories about Annie.

1922   Annie suffers severe injuries in an automobile accident.

1926   Annie dies on November 3. Frank dies November 21.

*AUTHOR'S NOTE: Nearly all young people's books about Annie Oakley put the date of her shooting match with Frank Butler in 1875 and her marriage to him in 1876. This book adopts later dates for several reasons.

1) Their marriage license is dated July 20, 1882.

2) In three separate newspaper articles in his later life, Frank claimed that the famous match occurred in the spring of 1881.

3) Author Shirl Kasper, who wrote a biography about Annie Oakley, did much of her research by reading newspapers that were published during that time. She concludes that Frank didn't even begin his shooting career until the mid-1870s.

4) In that era, it would have been very unusual for a girl to get married when she was only 15 or 16.

5) Since Annie didn't return to her family until sometime in 1875, it doesn't seem likely that she would have had enough time to become such a famous shooter. If she was 20 at the time of the match, she would have had plenty of time to establish her reputation. Everyone in the region would have known about her.

6) Annie's early life was difficult. She managed to overcome those difficulties. It is likely that she became a very self-confident young woman. It is hard to imagine how she could have waited more than six years to join her husband's act.

TIMELINE IN HISTORY

1826 Joseph-Nicéphore Niepce takes the first photograph.

1846 William F. "Buffalo Bill" Cody is born.

1850 Francis "Frank" E. Butler is born.

1860 Abraham Lincoln is elected president of the United States.

1869 The Union Pacific and Southern Pacific Railroads meet in Utah, completing the first rail line across the United States of America.

1876 Under the command of Sitting Bull and Crazy Horse, Lakota Sioux and Northern Cheyenne combined Indian forces to defeat U.S. Army Lieutenant Colonel George Custer at the Battle of Little Bighorn in Montana.

1901 Theodore Roosevelt, who helped to popularize shooting competitions, becomes president of the United States.

1903 Henry Ford founds the Ford Motor Company, which will mass-produce automobiles.

1917 Buffalo Bill Cody dies. The United States enters World War I.

1918 World War I ends.

1927 Philo T. Farnsworth shows the first working model of a television.

1939 World War II begins; it will last until 1945.

1951 Color television comes to the United States.

2006 Annie Oakley Festival Days in Darke County, Ohio, is held for the 42nd time.

FIND OUT MORE

Books

Hamilton, John. *Heroes and Villains of the Wild West: Annie Oakley.* Minneapolis: Abdo and Daughters, 1996.

Macy, Sue. *Bull's-Eye: A Photobiography of Annie Oakley.* Washington, D.C.: National Geographic Society, 2001.

Spinner, Stephanie. *Who Was Annie Oakley?* New York: Grosset and Dunlap, 2002.

Works Consulted

Del Sordo, Stephen G. "Annie Oakley" http://www.dorchesterlibrary.org/library/aoakley.html

Kasper, Shirl. *Annie Oakley.* Norman, Oklahoma: University of Oklahoma Press, 1992.

McMurtry, Larry. *The Colonel and Little Missie.* New York: Simon & Schuster, 2005.

Sorg, Eric V. "Annie Got Her Guns." *Wild West,* February 2001. http://thehistorynet.com/we/blannieoakley/

On the Internet

Annie Oakley Foundation http://www.annieoakleyfoundation.org/

Women in History "Annie Oakley." http://www.lkwdpl.org/wihohio/oakl-ann.htm

GLOSSARY

abandoned (uh-BAN-dund)—Left behind.

era (AY-ruh)—A time period characterized by a famous person or prominent feature.

frontier (frun-TEER)—An area between settled country and country that hasn't been developed.

game—Animals that people regularly hunt.

humiliated (hyoo-MIH-lee-ay-ted)—Very embarrassed.

infirmary (in-FUR-muh-ree)—A place where ill people or people without money are housed and taken care of.

media (MEE-dee-uh)—Systems used for communicating with many people, such as radio, newspapers, magazines.

retractions (ree-TRAK-shuns)—Statements that admit other statements are not true; retractions often also apologize for the untrue statements.

rumor (ROO-mur)—A story that probably isn't true but spreads anyway.

Sioux (SOO)—A famous group of Midwest Indian tribes.

spectacular (spek-TAK-yuh-lur)—Something very eye-catching and dramatic, often done on a large scale.

sued (SOOD)—Took a person to court to obtain money or an apology for doing something hurtful.

INDEX